Dogtags and Pearls 5

Lessons from Heaven

Katherine A. Sands

DEDICATION

These writings would not have come about without the influence of my spiritual mother and mentor, Shirley Duckworth. Without her, I wouldn't be where I am today. She was God's gift to me at a time when I needed a godly role model. She listened to my immature ranting, prayed for me when I was crazy, put up with me and loved me, even when she didn't want to. She encouraged me to journal my relationship with God. I love her dearly and treasure the friendship we have. She is a serious Kingdom builder and influence in her family, an intercessor and a rare gem in the church.

My friend and mentor went to Heaven on Monday, March 7, 2022. Her presence will be sorely missed. She was a true picture of Titus 2:3 and 4…how the older women are to teach the younger women in the church. This needs to come back to the Body of Christ as Titus instructed. We need spiritual mothers and fathers.

CONTENTS

Preface

I was lucky to get the domain name dogtagsandpearls.com. It only came to me the morning I put on my dog tag necklace with verses from Psalm 23 on it and decided to accompany it with pearl earrings. Hmmm....dogtags and pearls...the plain and the precious. It made me think about how people judge the outsides of people and miss the **precious** that is on the inside. We all do it. C'mon...you know you do. It's so easy to write people off by judging their appearance. But it's so wrong! There is something precious on the inside of every person. Our society has trained us to value exterior appearances to the point of obsession. Those who aren't "beautiful" or who have defects are brushed aside, given less consideration. I want to pay closer attention to those "lesser" people. I think Jesus would have too.

This is my fifth book in the series of the Dogtags and Pearls, Lessons From Heaven books. I didn't plan this. I started writing on the blog...and then one book was published, and then two. At the time, I didn't know there would be any more, but it looks like they will continue to come out because I'm still writing at dogtagsandpearls.com. The title comes from the idea of dog tags as a rough and plain adornment, where pearls are considered of high value and precious. Never judge a book by its cover, my grandmother always said, and she wasn't talking about books. You never know what "pearls" something plain might contain, be it books or people!

My desire in these essays is to encourage the reader's faith and stimulate a desire to serve the One who died to save us as well as feed your spirit with biblical revelations. May God use my stories to do so. (Except where indicated, all scripture references are from the NKJV.)

Katherine Sands

1. Jesus Working at Walmart

Have you run into shortages of food and other products during this government-sponsored hysteria called Covid? We humans get stuck on certain things we like, and my husband and I are no different. He likes Stax chips. They are better than Pringles in that they are less oily and a bit thicker, but they have been in short supply lately and I have been searching high and low for the sour cream and onion as those are my husband's favorites. He also loves the fruit punch Gatorade, and that too has disappeared from store shelves in our locality. I have been on the hunt for both for three to four weeks now. It could be that we are to simply move on to other products….but then the skies part and the sun comes out.

We were in another locality on the weekend and on Sunday afternoon, I went to a Walmart there to hunt for these items. I actually found two cans of the sour cream and onion Stax chips. Of course they were in the very back of very deep warehouse shelves, but I prevailed. So far, so good…now on to the Gatorade. I found some fruit punch! The small bottles come in a group of ten all strapped together in a plastic carrier. There were three of those on the shelf. The problem was, I could only reach one of them. The box with two more was just ever so slightly out of my reach, and I had exhausted the only option at the moment by standing on the bottom shelf to reach up there. All I could do was consider climbing up on the second shelf, which I wasn't too keen to do.

Enter an elderly man on a Walmart scooter. He came down the aisle while I was looking around to see if there was anything I could use to grab onto the little box that held the long sought after Gatorade. But there was nothing. He approached and said, "Maybe I can help."

Now remember, this man was easily in his 70s and perhaps even 80. He was riding a scooter…you know, the ones that people use who can't or don't walk. I had no idea what he had in mind, but he stood up slowly with a cane in his hand…a cane with a HOOK on it. He tried to grab the Gatorade with it, but kept scraping over the top of the bottles. I helped guide him until we could hook the edge of the box and bring it forward just enough where I could reach it. I was ecstatic, to say the least. This was all the fruit punch Gatorade there was on the shelf and I was determined to get it all. I thanked him profusely and then I said, "You are a Godsend!" And he replied, No I'm not. I'm just a guy who happened to be here."

Au contraire, my friend. You were my helper provided by Jesus at that exact moment to assist one of His kids. You just don't know it.

Now unto Him that is able to do exceeding abundantly above all that we ask or think, according to the power that works in us, to Him be the glory in the church and in Christ Jesus throughout all generations, forever and ever. Amen. ~Ephesians 3:20-21~~September 1, 2021

NOTES

2. The Devil is Dumber Than We Think

1 Corinthians 2:7-8 *"But we speak the wisdom of God in a mystery, the hidden wisdom which God ordained before the ages for our glory,* **Which none of the princes of this world knew: for had they known it, they would not have crucified the Lord of glory.**" The princes of the world this is talking about are the invisible rulers of darkness, who were also operating in people. Scriptures calls satan the prince of the power of the air. Ephesians 2:2

I'm kind of amazed the devil couldn't figure this out. Let's think about it. In Genesis, when God started handing out the consequences for Adam and Eve's sin, we see God announcing "I'm gonna send Someone." (my paraphrase) Speaking to the devil in Genesis 3:15, God says, *"And I will put enmity between you and the woman, and between your seed and her Seed; He shall bruise your head, and you shall bruise His heel."* One would think the devil knew God well enough to know He meant what He said.

In Isaiah 7:14, God again gave a clue: *"Therefore the Lord Himself will give you a sign: Behold, the virgin shall conceive and bear a Son, and shall call His name Immanuel."* So a good detective on the trail of a mystery would have seen that and been looking for that event. Maybe he wasn't paying attention. Maybe he had a day off! Maybe he was sleeping.

There were other clues in the Old Testament that point to the One Who would bruise satan's head.

I think we see the devil missing it in Daniel 9 when Daniel was praying and the angel was able to get the answer to Daniel immediately. That revelation is a totally awesome bit of prophetic information of what would happen in the end times. But in Daniel 10, we see Daniel again praying, but this time the angel was opposed for three weeks before he could get the answer to the prophet. I think the devil woke up after seeing what happened in Daniel 9 and realized he had to stop Daniel's answers to prayer.

For 4000 years, the devil watched man use blood sacrifices to cover sin as God had instructed them. Four thousand years! You would think he might have figured it out. The pattern was clearly laid out. For over four thousand years, satan had control and free rein over man in the earth. He was the ruler. He was the king basically over men, except where men had faith in God and a covenant, which afforded them protection from the works of darkness. But God had said, I'm gonna send Someone who will bruise your head. The devil is stupid and should have believed God. But arrogance deceives…

God kept that promise. The blood sacrifices to cover sin continued for over 4000 years….until Jesus, an innocent man came and died for our sins. The devil still didn't have it figured out. In his arrogance and madness, perhaps even insanity, he overplayed his hand and killed an innocent man Who was the Son of God and could not be held by death. The devil illegally claimed the life of an innocent Man. God's plan always had been for Jesus to come, live a sinless life, demonstrate what the kingdom of God was like, and then die; this would take all the devil's power from him and give authority over the earth back to God's regenerated humans.

This was God's original plan from the foundation of the world.

It's hard to believe the devil couldn't figure that out…he is way dumber than we think. His power has been stripped from him. God is WAY smarter than he is. Remember that.

Colossians 2:14-15 "*…having wiped out the handwriting of requirements that was against us, which was contrary to us. And He has taken it out of the way, having nailed it to the cross. Having disarmed principalities and powers, He made a public spectacle of them, triumphing over them in it.*" – September 25, 2021

NOTES

3. If We Think Wrong, We Act Wrong

I have probably said this before on this blog: We were created to become the image of something. Watch a child mimic his or her parents. It's what we do.

When we are young innocent babes, we are a blank slate, we neither know who we are nor what we are supposed to do in this thing called life. If our parents are not saved people, they don't know who they are either! They are floundering in this world. We become what we see. I remember not wanting to be like my mother, but I was doing the exact same things she did even though she didn't raise me.

Parenthood is spiritual. Children are given spiritual assignments, depending on what the parent has allowed into the child's life. So parents impart a spiritual life to their babies, whether for good or bad, whether they know it or not. *"Train up a child in the way he should go. And when he is old he will not depart from it."* Proverbs 22:6

Iniquities, sins, and wrong ways of thinking are spiritually visited on subsequent generations. Exodus 20:5 *"Thou shalt not bow down thyself to them, nor serve them: for I the LORD thy God am a jealous God, visiting the iniquity of the fathers upon the children unto the third and fourth generation of them that hate me;"* I didn't say it; God did.

So we are what we think we are. Does that sound about right? Many times, we are what our parents said we are. We act on what we believe. We usually don't act on things we don't believe, correct? So we are following what we ourselves believe, as a rule.

The bible says, as a man thinks in his heart, so is he. Proverbs 23:7. So our thinking and our acting are very much intertwined. Coming to Jesus causes a change to begin in our hearts, which affects our thinking. We start to acknowledge we NEED God. That's where all change begins.

So if the way you think makes you an unhappy person, what is the answer? I'm amazed at how long people can live being unhappy, which means their thoughts are unhappy. More than likely, their own self-image is unhappy.

Perhaps I have a very low threshold for pain; I was fairly young when I decided I must be doing something wrong. My life was not going the way I wanted it to. I decided there must be another way. I began to surrender to God then, realizing I didn't have good answers or any answers at all on my own. What I was doing (sin) was not working for me. I began searching, looking for help. And that is where God met with me.

Man is God's crowning creation. He has been uniquely given the power and authority to rule over the earth and creation, even independently from God the Creator. Man is supposed to be ruling the earth for good. Of all of God's creation, man is the only one with this ability, the ability to reason. Animals are instinctual, without the ability to reason. But man apart from God becomes beast-like, only making decisions based on his own selfish desires and not on logical reason. Isn't that what we are seeing today in our society? Especially now during this time of Covid. It seems all logic and reasoning have been thrown out the window, even in the world of medicine.

What continues to amaze me is how long humans are able to persist in their wrong thinking, even when it makes them miserable and produces bad results. They will continue to do the same things over and over, even though they do not prosper in it. They are not happy, but they continue in it, day after day as if there is no other way. Why do we hold on to it?

I heard a teaching once about how the brain has pathways in it that are there from continued use, just like a worn path through the woods. And when the brain is confronted with a choice, it will always go toward the old pathway that it has always chosen. We might term it the default position. It takes effort for the brain (and the person) to create new pathways that will become the ones it relies on in the future, but the bible says we are to not be *"conformed to the world, but to be renewed in the spirit of our minds."* Romans 12:2.

We now have access to the mind of God, to think like He thinks! Thoughts of faith and hope and love. But we have to make the choice to do that. We must choose to reject the old ways of thinking and embrace the new. 1 Corinthians 2. We must renew our minds by praying and mediating on the thoughts of God. And His thoughts are in His word, so that is where we must go if we are to learn new ways of thinking and thereby create new pathways in our brains, a new default position, so to speak.

God says in 2 Timothy 1:7 that He *"has not given us a spirit of fear, but of power love and a sound mind."* If we accept that as true (and we should), we have to embrace that promise as our own, agree with it, and determine to lay hold of it for

ourselves. That is how we obtain every promise God says in
His word.

If we can truly change those old pathways in our brain (and
we can), there is a whole new perspective awaiting us, one full
of joy and peace, no matter what is happening around us.
With joy and peace operating in our hearts and minds, instead
of fear, we can make right decisions, right choices. We have
the right perspective. Heaven has come and taken a place in
our lives!~~September 25, 2021

NOTES

4. Marking Memorials To God

Why do we have Memorial Day? Fourth of July? Columbus Day, President's Day, etc.? Why do we humans mark days, times and seasons?

I believe it's because humans have short memories. We don't need to live in the past, but we do need to remember events. Our history is how we learn. You know the saying, "Those who forget history are doomed to repeat it." I believe that to be true.

In the Old Testament, as God was forming His nation of God-minded people, He instructed them to make memorials. These were places where certain events in the life of the nation happened. This marking or remembrance of events would cause them to remember what happened and to instruct their children, so that the children would know the history of their people. The story of the Israelites leaving Egypt is recounted every year at Passover. In Exodus 12:14, Moses instructed the people to build an altar of stones at Mount Sinai to commemorate their covenant with God. In Joshua 4, they were instructed to pick up stones as they crossed the Jordan going into the Promised Land so they could build a memorial to that event. They were instructed to never forget the Lord Who had delivered them.

The history of a people gives identity and direction. It's a bit like families. The mother and dad and the whole family history identifies where you come from, and something about who you are. Children should never to be constrained by that, whether for good or bad, but it's a history that is important. It is identity.

In the Christian life today, our marking of memorials is our personal stories of our encounters with God, where we see Him working on our behalf. These stories are important. When hard times come, difficult places, we can look back and remember....our God has always been with us, even when we forget, but the stories of our encounters with Him and His care, where He rescued us or came through for us in dire situations, remind us and give us hope and faith. I used to sit and watch the 700 Club and the stories of people who had been healed made me cry as my heart was touched by the demonstration of God's love for people. It is truly amazing! Those stories are also for those who may not be believers yet as it gives them hope too. That's why we are to always be ready to give a reason to others for the hope that is in us, as 1 Peter 3:15 tells us. Our stories give other people hope too. What God has done for us, He will do for others.

At Christmas, we mark the birth of Jesus. Perhaps it's not really His birthday, but we mark it. I'm not sure it really matters that it may not be the right date. We mark it every year. We set aside time, a season, to celebrate the fact that God sent His Son as a baby to come and live on the earth…all for US! That is indeed something to celebrate!

But when the fullness of the time had come, God sent forth His Son, born of a woman, born under the law, to redeem those who were under the law, that we might receive the adoption as sons. ~~ Galatians 4:4-5

God Himself came to live under the law of Moses, those
written rules and requirements which He had given to men.
By this time, men were well aware they could not meet the
law's requirements. They needed a Savior, someone who
could keep the law FOR them, and that is what Jesus did. God
is no longer imputing man's sins against them. All of His
wrath against sin was satisfied in the sacrifice and death of
our Lord and Savior Jesus Christ.

2 Corinthians 5:19 *"that God was in Christ reconciling the world
to Himself, not imputing their trespasses to them,…"* We celebrate
that sacrifice at the season of Easter. And that, my friends, is
very good news! ~~September 25, 2021

NOTES

5. In The Kingdom

…"Your Kingdom come, Your will be done, on earth as it is in Heaven." What did Jesus mean when He said to pray this way?

In Heaven, or the Kingdom, there is complete healing, complete wellness, no sickness, no disease. We see this demonstrated in Jesus's life, as He is *"the radiance of God's glory and the exact representation of his being, sustaining all things by his powerful word. After he had provided purification for sins, he sat down at the right hand of the Majesty in heaven"* Hebrews 1:3. Jesus *"went about doing good and healing all who were oppressed of the devil for God was with Him."* Acts 10:38

In God's Kingdom there is light, no darkness, complete understanding of truth, no lie, no deception. These are works of satan and he does not dwell there. Jesus, the Way, the Truth and the Life, reigns over all and has seated us with Him in the heavenly places, if we have accepted His payment for our sins.

In the Kingdom all needs are fulfilled, no one lacks; it is perfection as in the Garden of Eden before Adam sinned and lost access to it.

Isaiah 11:6-9 speaks of a future time…
The earth will be filled with the knowledge of the Lord as:

The wolf will live with the lamb,
*   the leopard will lie down with the goat,*
the calf and the lion and the yearling together;
*   and a little child will lead them.*
The cow will feed with the bear,
*   their young will lie down together,*
*   and the lion will eat straw like the ox.*
The infant will play near the cobra's den,
*   and the young child will put its hand into the viper's nest.*
They will neither harm nor destroy
*   on all my holy mountain,*
for the earth will be filled with the knowledge of the Lord
*   as the waters cover the sea.*

Isaiah 65-17-25 describes the new earth when the Kingdom of God rules over it.

"See, I will create
*   new heavens and a new earth.*
The former things will not be remembered,
*   nor will they come to mind.*
18 But be glad and rejoice forever
*   in what I will create,*
for I will create Jerusalem to be a delight
*   and its people a joy.*
19 I will rejoice over Jerusalem
*   and take delight in my people;*
the sound of weeping and of crying
*   will be heard in it no more.*
20 "Never again will there be in it
*   an infant who lives but a few days,*
*   or an old man who does not live out his years;*
the one who dies at a hundred
*   will be thought a mere child;*
the one who fails to reach a hundred
*   will be considered accursed.*
21 They will build houses and dwell in them;

they will plant vineyards and eat their fruit.
²² No longer will they build houses and others live in them,
*   or plant and others eat.*
For as the days of a tree,
*   so will be the days of my people;*
my chosen ones will long enjoy
*   the work of their hands.*
²³ They will not labor in vain,
*   nor will they bear children doomed to misfortune;*
for they will be a people blessed by the Lord,
*   they and their descendants with them.*
²⁴ Before they call I will answer;
*   while they are still speaking I will hear.*
²⁵ The wolf and the lamb will feed together,
*   and the lion will eat straw like the ox,*
*   and dust will be the serpent's food.*
They will neither harm nor destroy
*   on all my holy mountain,"*
says the Lord.

These passages describe a time in the future when the Kingdom of God will rule on the earth. Sounds great, doesn't it? At the present time, we do not see this reality, but we are to continually advance towards it with our prayers, "Your Kingdom come, Your will be done on earth as it is in Heaven." In this manner, we advance and occupy the places God has given to us.

Jesus only did what He saw the Father doing and said what He heard the Father say. If that is true, and it is (John 5:19 and John 12:49), then Heaven, or perfection, is the will of God for the earth too. If we are disciples of Jesus, we are to pray "Your kingdom come, Your will be done on earth as it is in Heaven." That's what He taught His disciples. Yes, I know it doesn't look like that is happening at the moment. And complete perfection will never be reached because man is not perfect, but we have grace through Jesus Christ.

So, those of us who are believers must do battle to bring Heaven to earth every day then. That is the will of God. Hebrews 10:9, referring to the Old Testament Psalms 45:8, speaks of this regarding Jesus. "See, here I am; I have come to do Your will." We as believers are to make Heaven come to earth first in our own lives, then we are able to influence others with Heaven as we live out the principles of the Kingdom. We are to be the aroma, the fragrance of Christ, the bible says. *"For we are to God the fragrance of Christ among those who are being saved and among those who are perishing."* 2 Corinthians 2:15.

We are the "salt" that gives the earth its "flavor" the scriptures say. We ought not to lose that…*"You are the salt of the earth; but if the salt loses its flavor, how shall it be seasoned? It is then good for nothing but to be thrown out and trampled underfoot by men."* Matthew 5:13.

Pray this way! "Your kingdom come, Your will be done on earth as it is in Heaven." Let Your Kingdom come, Lord Jesus! We are willing! ~ September 28, 2021

NOTES

6. Only Be Strong and Courageous; Do Not Fear

Joshua 1:6-9 *"Only be strong and very courageous, that you may observe to do according to all the law which Moses My servant commanded you; do not turn from it to the right hand or to the left, that you may prosper wherever you go. This Book of the Law shall not depart from your mouth, but you shall meditate in it day and night, that you may observe to do according to all that is written in it. For then you will make your way prosperous, and then you will have good success. Have I not commanded you? Be strong and of good courage; do not be afraid, nor be dismayed, for the Lord your God is with you wherever you go."*

Just as Joshua and the nation of Israel went in to conquer territory that was ruled by evil men, that land of prosperity and blessing that God had promised was theirs, we the church also have territory to take in our day. We have ceded ground in our nation in government, in schools, in society at large. Everywhere we turn, there is darkness where lying and cheating reigns. There is no fear of God. It seems that most men "do what is right in their own eyes" and the thoughts of men are on evil continually, as in the days of Noah, when the flood came and destroyed all of the evil on the earth.

Those living in darkness today think nothing of destroying government property and records, denying and obfuscating requests for information to those assigned oversight, stealing taxpayer's money by submitting false receipts and overcharging simple tasks. Government officials don't give it a second thought. Your money is their money, right? They have become arrogant and are now rulers instead of servants. Is it because we have not demanded it of them? Are we compliant? I think to some degree we, the people must be. The church of our time is the standard-bearer. Are we holding a standard that is righteous, that is against darkness and gives light to our society?

We are not helpless, because we have the Word of God and the Spirit of God, but do we understand the authority that has been invested in the church by Jesus? He is waiting until His enemies are made His footstool, Hebrews 10:13 says. How will His enemies be made his footstool? He already defeated the devil's power on the cross. He opened the way for His church to live in the light and not in darkness. Then He gave authority over demonic powers to His followers so they can set others free. The Church is His Body today in the earth and is to co-labor with Jesus in implementing the plan to make His enemies His footstool. How do we do this? By using the authority He gave us.

He said I give you the keys of the Kingdom, (Matthew 16:19) whatever you bind on earth is bound in heaven, and occupy until I come (Luke 19:13). His sent His disciples out to cast out demons, heal the sick, and raise the dead. This was their training. They came back rejoicing that devils were subject to them. They liked this authority. We have that same authority. God has given it to us, but are we using it to change the world we live in as the early disciples did? I fear we are not, and the current condition of our world is evidence that demons are having their way and God's people are failing to challenge them sufficiently.

We are equipped for this battle. We are all here "for such a time as this." We win if we don't quit. But in order to do so, we must know two things. We must know who we are in Christ and we must know what this authority is that Jesus has given to us to overcome evil and set spiritual captives free.

I have written much in previous posts about our identity in Christ, how the sinless Jesus took on Himself our sins, and then imputed to us His own sinless right standing with God. That gives us identity and confidence in our relationship with God. We must know that. It is a most important part of our "spiritual armor."

This identity made the 17-year-old sheepherder David able to go out and take on the giant Goliath with confidence. Because David had spent time with God, he had confidence that he could take down Goliath ….and we can too, no matter how big and hopeless things appear. We have been given authority over darkness. We are to use it. Let's be engaged so that Jesus' death is not in vain.

It looks like the devil is in charge, but he is not actually. We the church are! The only answer to our dilemma is a return to God in our land. It is coming! Let all of us in these times be engaged in finding and doing the will of God.

Dear Jesus, I present myself to you as a living sacrifice, ready to serve Your purposes in the earth in these times. Help me to understand what You need of me. I commit to seek You with all my heart because I only trust Your desires for me. Fill me with Your Holy Spirit that I may have the power to be Your influence in the earth and build Your Kingdom. – October 19, 2021

NOTES

7. David Ran Toward His Goliath

Recently, as I have been pondering what looks to be "giant" problems in our society, my attention has come to the story of David, the anointed king of Israel from the book of 1 Samuel.

David was 17 years old, and the youngest of his father's eight sons when he was anointed by the prophet Samuel to be the successor to Saul, king of Israel. So David had a *promise* of being king, but he was not king yet. Instead, David spent his days tending to his father's sheep while several of his brothers went off to fight for Israel in King Saul's army. The story starts in 1 Samuel 16.

But there came a time when David, the young shepherd boy, went to take food to his brothers in the army and found them in a standoff with a giant named Goliath and his army. The army of Israel was deathly afraid of engaging with the giant as the scriptures say he was around nine feet tall. But Goliath kept taunting them, challenging them to send someone out to fight him.

When David saw all of this, his response was, "Who is this uncircumcised Philistine that he should defy the armies of the living God?" You see, David knew his identity. David knew he belonged to the armies of the living God because he had been spending time out on the hillside with the sheep and with his God. David was a worshipper of God. Therefore he knew who he was. This was the difference between David and the armies of Israel.

As the story continues, David is given the opportunity to engage the "giant" with unconventional weapons because he could not use conventional ones, such as armor and the like. There was a reward offered, with all kinds of riches, tax relief, and the opportunity to marry the king's daughter, so it's possible these things weighed into his decision to engage, but I am more inclined to believe that his righteous anger was so great, anger at the fact that evil was intimidating God's people was most likely his highest motivator to engage in what looked to the natural eye like a losing battle. I'm sure he could not fathom that God's people were actually afraid of this "uncircumcised Philistine" who had no covenant with God. I'm sure David was aware that fear of giants is what kept the first group of Israelites wandering in the wilderness for 40 years before they went in and took the Promised land. But what speaks to me at this point in time is, the scripture says David RAN towards Goliath. David didn't just jump around assessing what advantage he had like men do in a boxing ring. David had the plan already. Had God spoken it to him? It would seem so. David ran towards Goliath with five smooth stones and his slingshot. He knew what he was going to do. It was never really going to be hand to hand combat! All he needed was one well-placed rock…

Goliath never saw it coming.

It is written in the scriptures, and I have quoted it elsewhere on this blog, *"if the rulers of this age had known, they would not have crucified the Lord of glory."* In other words, if they had known what God's plan was for the salvation and the restoration of men back to God's original plan, they would not have crucified Jesus. They walked into God's trap. If Goliath had known what the plan was, he might have run away from David instead of walking into the same trap. You see, the devil doesn't know everything….God has plans that are hidden from him. Aren't you glad about that?

I believe we are seeing the same things happening in our society. First, President Trump, in his administration, came out and challenged the powers of darkness in the political world. They hated him for it. He, being one man, was only able to achieve so much, but now….he has inspired many, as populations around the entire world are rising up and challenging our current "Goliath." Oh, you may not hear about it if you are still listening to the mainstream media because they won't report it, but it is happening. The Church needs to engage this "Goliath," which is the current worldwide effort to censor, oppress, and take freedom away from all of mankind. The Church has the spiritual weapons of war to win, and a covenant with God. And we are destined to win, just like David did. He took the head off his Goliath. We just need to "follow the plan." Each of us has a part to play in this.

Stay tuned in to God and pray. The word of God and the Spirit of God have the plan. The scriptures and the stories of those who have gone before us help direct our journey.

"all scripture is given by inspiration of god, and is profitable for doctrine, for reproof, for correction, for instruction in righteousness,… 2 Timothy 3:16.

Dear Jesus, on our own, we cannot know the plan to defeat the enemies in our world today. We rest in the defeat you accomplished by dying for us and bringing us into Your kingdom of Light. We need your help every moment of the day if we are to bring light to those around us. We thank you and rely on You for all wisdom and knowledge of what You would have us do. – November 24, 2021

NOTES

8. What's That About Destiny?

Our ultimate, forever destiny is Heaven. If you have experienced salvation and the cleansing of your sins, you will live eternally in all of Heaven's perfections and beauty. We are His beloved and we will spend eternity with our Lover King. But what about now? While we are here on the earth, what are we supposed to be doing? This is a huge question. It involves finding our purpose and place in His kingdom plans. Salvation is just the starting place.

After Jesus's death and resurrection, when He met with His disciples, He gave them final instructions. He wasn't taking them with Him. And He doesn't take us out of the earth either after we get saved. That's because God has something for each of us to do here and it is our responsibility to find out what that is. At the same time, we are stuck dealing with a devil, a force who opposes everything we are and everything we do. He opposes all that is good. So why are we left here with him? Why has he been left here with us? (At its simplest, one reason might be that without opposition, we have nothing to overcome.)

From the beginning in Genesis, God promised to send a Savior to mankind in order to bring them back to His original intent, which was to "be fruitful and multiply, fill the earth and subdue it; have dominion over…" everything. After the man and woman disobeyed God, thereby giving satan authority over the earth, God said to the serpent in Genesis

3:15 *"And I will put enmity between you and the woman, And between your seed and her Seed; He shall bruise your head, And you shall bruise His heel."* (Most believers understand the serpent to be inspired or even perhaps inhabited by the spirit that opposes God, which is the devil. This passage was the first one that foretells his future at the hands of the Son of God.)

The Old Testament is full of shadows, prophecies, and evidences that God was sending Someone to rescue mankind. Today, we live in that reality. He has come, He has saved us and rescued us from the devil and the power of sin. We no longer have to sin. We are now free from its power. We are redeemed and regenerated humans, with the Holy Spirit of God living inside of us. God was WITH the Old Testament saints, but now He is IN us.

We have dominion over the unseen spiritual forces arrayed against us. We have spiritually been raised up and seated with Jesus our King into the heavenly places because of His sacrifice. Ephesians 2:4-6 *"But God who is rich in mercy, because of His great love with which He loved us, even when we were dead in trespasses, made us alive together with Christ , (by grace you have been saved), and raised us up together, and made us sit together in the heavenly places in Christ Jesus."*

We have been restored to God's original intent. We are now kings and priests unto our God. Revelation 5:10 *"And have made us kings and priests to our God; And we shall reign on the earth."*

He took our sin nature and gave us His righteousness. We have changed jurisdictions. We still live in the earth realm, but we are now citizens of Heaven. Jesus came and defeated the devil on our behalf. John 3:8, and then said to His disciples, *"The works that I do, you shall do also, and even greater things shall you do."* John 14:12. That's pretty intense. Well, are we doing the works He did? And what about the greater works?

There are specific things that we have been created to do. This is a plan that God Himself created and appointed for us. We need to find that plan. We cannot find fulfillment until we do. There is nothing more fulfilling on this planet than serving Him in the capacity that He appointed for us. We are gifted with talents and abilities to do the particular task that He appointed for us to do in the earth. Jeremiah 1:5 says that Jeremiah's appointment in the earth was foreordained. So it is with us also. That scripture is worth reading and pondering.

Jeremiah 1:5 *"Before I formed you in the womb I knew you; Before you were born I sanctified you; I ordained you a prophet to the nations."* All of us have a destiny here on the earth, a task to accomplish.

Ephesians 2:10 *"For we are His workmanship, created in Christ Jesus for good works, which God prepared beforehand that we should walk in them."*

We are Christ's ambassadors, (2 Cor. 5:20) kept here after our salvation experience to spread the news of His love and represent Him on the earth. We are to show unbelievers His character and love. This is a general sense of God's plan for all of us. The world needs to see the love of God now more than ever. The number of broken families with children who do not know the love of God has greatly increased in these times and have contributed much to the breakdown of our society. People do not know God loves them, hence they do not know their identity. We are to let the light of God shine in our lives, so that people see it and hopefully will surrender to Him for salvation, assured that He really does love and accept them unconditionally.

The leaders in our churches should be helping their people find the plan of God for their lives, according to their gifting and talents, and help them each reach the fullest measure of why they are here, so that we can be about fulfilling His plan for the earth, affecting our society, and indeed hastening His coming!

2 Peter 3:11-12 *"Therefore, since all these things will be dissolved, what manner of persons ought you to be in holy conduct and godliness, looking for and hastening the coming of the day of God, because of which the heavens will be dissolved, being on fire, and the elements will melt with fervent heat?"* – November 25, 2021

NOTES

9. Taking Every Thought Captive, Part 1

"For the weapons of our warfare are not carnal but mighty in God for pulling down strongholds, casting down arguments and every high thing that exalts itself against the knowledge of God, bringing every thought into captivity to the obedience of Christ…"
2 Corinthians 10:4-5.

The apostle Paul wrote this letter to the Corinthians. I dare say this passage of scripture is not for the casual believer, but demonstrates the sold out love attitude of the apostle who was determined to fulfill the will of God for his life and to be the best representation of Jesus in his world. We too can adopt this same attitude. I believe this is the mindset of the believer who pursues God with his whole heart, always waiting and watching for the Lord's direction and action, one who listens closely, because he knows he needs answers from Heaven in order to navigate life. The fact remains…we do not know everything, no matter how smart we are.

It is written in Psalm 103:7 *"He made known His ways to Moses, His acts to the children of Israel.* Israel knew God's acts, but Moses knew his ways. What's the difference?

Does that describe you today? You know God's acts, you've heard of Him, you have *heard* that He does great things for people, but do you know His ways? Have you experienced

these things? Knowing His ways takes time in His presence.
Moses knew God's ways because he spent time with God in
the tent of meeting, getting to know God. That is what we
must do also to know His ways. We can know Him like Moses
did. We have a much better covenant with God in this age
than Moses did. God desires us to know Him intimately.

If you did not actually live with your husband or wife or
children, but observed their lives from a distance, you would
only know what they do, which is not the same as an intimate
relationship with them, living beside them day after day,
where you get to see closely what makes them tick, what their
personality is. You would only know their ways if you lived
intimately with them.

We are instructed by this same apostle to *renew our minds* in
the book of Romans. *"And do not be conformed to this world, but
be transformed by the renewing of your mind, that you may prove
what is that good and acceptable and perfect will of God.* Romans
12:2. The promise is that when we renew our minds, we will
find the will of God! We can change our thinking, and we
ought to!

Before salvation, our minds have been trained by the world
and the devil. We believed lies. Once God's Spirit comes to
dwell in us through the baptism of the Holy Spirit, we are
connected to His mind, His thoughts. Our thinking changes as
we study His word and spend time with Him.

I believe that, in the times that we live in, it is more imperative
than ever that we guard our minds and "take every thought
captive to the obedience of Christ" and His word, in order to
avoid the deception and lies that are out there. *"Be sober, be
vigilant; because your adversary the devil walks about like a roaring
lion, seeking whom he may devour."* 1 Peter 5:8.

Witness the bizarre behavior of some who occupy our current world. It is evidence to me that deception has taken a major leap forward and those who are not committed to truth are falling for lies in a huge way. It is clear a major division among the population is taking place, a division between those who will believe the lie and those who will not. In a world that has decided there are no absolutes, we must be absolutely committed to the truth found in the word of God in these times if we are to avoid gross deception.

Dear Jesus, our world is quickly changing and, at least for the moment, does not appear to be heading in the right direction. We place our confidence in You as the only answer to our dilemma. We commit to pursuing You and the knowledge of Your Word as the only place to find answers. I welcome Your Holy Spirit to come into my life and be my Teacher in all things. I expect You to tell me all things I need to know as You have promised. Psalm 119:105 says Your word is a lamp unto my feet, and a light unto my path. I trust it above all things. I pray for Your light in changing my thoughts when they do not glorify You. I love You Jesus and thank You for everything You have done. – November 26, 2021

NOTES

10. Taking Every Thought Captive, Part 2

"For the weapons of our warfare are not carnal but mighty in God for pulling down strongholds, casting down arguments and every high thing that exalts itself against the knowledge of God, bringing every thought into captivity to the obedience of Christ…"
2 Corinthians 10:4-5.

In the last post I talked about intimacy as the way to know how God thinks. Much like living day to day with a spouse or a child, one learns how that person thinks when they spend time with them. Intimacy is the key to knowing the ways of God and the thoughts of God.

There is statement that lots of people make, whether Christian or not, that "God works in mysterious ways." The Lord says in His word *"For as the heavens are higher than the earth, So are My ways higher than your ways, And My thoughts than your thoughts.* Isaiah 55:8-9. If God's ways are mysterious, it is because of what this passage says. We don't think like God. How could we, with finite minds who do not know everything as He does? He knows everything about everyone, as well as the future. So yes, based on who He is in comparison to us, His ways would be mysterious…

But I would submit there may be other reasons people use this saying and it could be they can shrug off things as unknowable and therefore investigate it no further. But I don't believe that was ever God's intent or desire. If it was, what are we to do with statements such as these? *"You know all things and have no need for anyone to teach you?* 1 John 2:27. Or this one: *"Now I call you friends, because a servant does not know what his master is doing, but I call you friends, because I have freely told you all things. I have revealed everything to you from my father."* John 15:15. Intimacy is being shouted out in these passages.

God's desire that we understand Him and His kingdom is plainly expressed in the Gospels from Jesus himself. However, He did make a distinction between people. When asked, Why do you speak in parables? He said to His disciples (who asked why), *"Because it has been given to you to know the mysteries of the kingdom of heaven, but to them it has not been given."* Matthew 13:11. Disciples are those who spend time with Jesus, who ask questions. These get to know the mysteries. We may not understand everything, but we can have understanding of many things about Him and His ways. If you need answers, He has them!

The truth may be that many of us are like the Israelites at Mt. Sinai, when the mountain quaked and a fire was on it. The people said to Moses, you hear from God for us, we don't want to hear from Him for ourselves. They wanted a mediator because they were afraid of God. After all he had done for them in the wilderness journey, providing all of their food and water, and rescue from their enemies, they were still afraid of Him. He proved His goodness, but they were unable to appreciate it and their hearts did not change. He delivered them from the Egyptians with mighty displays of power, but they continued to resort to their natural thinking.

As an example, I know a person who once told me she didn't have time to read the word of God, that she was fed by the pastor once or twice a week. It seemed she expected the pastor to hear from God and tell her what He was saying, just like the Israelites in the wilderness. You see it was always God's intent that the entire nation of the Israelites be priests to Him and to hear from Him, each one for themselves. But they refused.

Psalm 23:2 says, speaking of the shepherd, "*He makes me to lie down in green pastures; He leads me beside the still waters.*" Green pastures speaks of the place to get nourishment, while water speaks of quenching thirst. Sheep are grazers, feeding on grassland, pasture, rangelands, and lawns.

The implication is the shepherd shows you a nourishing place to eat, to rest, and to drink, but the sheep must do the eating. The shepherd cannot do the eating for you. You yourself must desire the pure word of God. You must partake of it. The shepherd can only show you a place of nourishment. And that place is always the word of God. The Lord wants all of His people to partake of His word for themselves.

The thinking that "God works in mysterious ways" is a THOUGHT that stands guard and can keep one from having to inquire any further. We can be lazy. If it's too hard, many do not wish to pursue it. "God works in mysterious ways" can be a way to rationalize not pursuing the truth! This will shut you out of blessings! If you come near to God, He will come near to you. God wants you to know things. He wants you to think like He thinks. This is what 2 Corinthians 10:4-5 is talking about.

As an example of renewing your mind….there was a situation in my life that did not look like it would turn out as I had hoped. It was one where I believed the Lord was leading me. The first thought that came to my mind was an old familiar one that everyone knows: "If it seems to good to be true, then it probably isn't." But then I had this thought: *"Every good gift and every perfect gift is from above, and comes down from the Father of lights, with whom there is no variation or shadow of turning."* This is found in James 1:17.

I decided to discard the first thought and place my hope in the second one from James. That is how you renew your mind, by making the choice to believe the word of God. God will help you! – November 26, 2021

NOTES

11. My 2021 Birthday/God With Us

A couple of friends visited me last night on my birthday while I was in the throes of a tooth infection. These were not like Job's friends, who tried to explain to him why he was having so much trouble in life. These were friends bearing gifts. One brought me a Mexican dinner (yum), while the other brought dessert (double yum).

Before they left, one of my friends noticed a picture on my wall and asked what it was. It is a print of the Israelites' wilderness tabernacle with the nation camped around it. The glory of God is seen coming down over the inner court of the tabernacle.

A little background is called for. My husband and I saw this print some 25 plus years ago at some friends' home and fell in love with it. We were unable to cajole them out of it, but several years later a ministry had it for sale at a church I was attending and I bought that $15 print.

Because we loved it so much, we spent probably around $100 matting and framing it in regal fashion and it has hung on our walls ever since. One year I was doing some cleaning and looked at it closer. I was surprised that in all the years we had it, I had never noticed the people standing in front of their tents watching the glory of God come down over that tabernacle.

What does this picture of the wilderness tabernacle have to do with us today? It tells us something important about our Creator God. To my heart, the print depicts how MUCH God desires to be with His people. How else can one explain the great lengths God has gone to achieve that? If you go read about the tabernacle, it was a huge endeavor, with the people giving of their time and talents and wealth (which was actually plundered from Egypt when they left) to create it, set it up, then take it down, carry it with them, only to set it up again at a new campsite. It was a portable tabernacle, but it signified the presence of God with them. That depiction of the glory of God takes on greater meaning when one realizes that that glory is what now lives inside of us who believe. To read about that first tabernacle, see Exodus 25-27. (Side note: It is my opinion that camping is a lot of work anyway.)

Here at the Christmas season as we celebrate the birth of our Lord and Savior Jesus Christ, we are reminded of the desire of our God to dwell with us. *"Behold, the virgin shall be with child, and bear a Son, and they shall call His name Immanuel," which is translated, "God with us."* Matthew 1:23

Remember that, before God was separated from His creation by Adam and Eve's disobedience, He freely walked and talked with them in the Garden of Eden. After they gave their God-delegated dominion over the earth to the devil, they were separated from Him by that rebellion. As one teacher puts it, they essentially "kicked God out of the garden," thereafter siding with satan and bringing his curse upon the earth and mankind. Even nature is affected by it. Ever since that time, God provided a way to cover sin through animal sacrifices in the Jewish temple and get back into some sort of fellowship with his created humans. This effort finally culminated 4000 years later "in the fullness of time." Galatians 4:4 *"But when the fullness of the time had come, God sent forth His Son, born of a woman, born under the law."* God's Son Jesus was born in the likeness of man as Philippians 2:7 says of Jesus, *"but made Himself of no reputation, taking the form of a bondservant, and coming in the likeness of men."* John 1:14 says *"And the Word became flesh and dwelt among us, and we beheld His glory, the glory as of the only begotten of the Father, full of grace and truth.'*

The Word, Who is Jesus, came in the flesh to dwell among us, choosing not to sin and give the devil place, (unlike Adam) and to demonstrate the original intent of God, and the character and love of God through healing sickness and disease, casting demons out of people and doing good to all. He is called the second Adam, a true depiction of the freedom that God originally intended for His created beings; then He went on to suffer and die as the innocent and sinless sacrifice for all of our sins, past, present and future, on the cross. He was raised from the dead because death could not hold Him as He had no sin. Satan illegally killed Him. The plan was hidden from him, *"which none of the rulers of this age knew; for had they known, they would not have crucified the Lord of glory."*1 Cor. 2:8. God tricked the devil, because he is just not that smart…not as smart as God.

God's Son freely laid down His life to save us. This made the way for us to boldly access the presence of God. Read Hebrews 9 and 10 for a very good description of the first tabernacle, the sacrifices of the Old Testament and how that is all changed now that our new High Priest Jesus offered Himself once and for all and taken away our sins forever, hallelujah! Now God can once again have open fellowship with His creation, which was always His desire.

I would submit, is it possible God is a bit lonely? He is perfect in Himself, but His longing to dwell with us is depicted in the Old Testament with the establishment of that first tabernacle in the wilderness and the subsequent temples in Israel. In the present day New Testament reality, He actually dwells within us who believe!

He is the only Person in the universe in His unique category as Creator. The scriptures speak of the church being a bride for His Son Jesus. We are intended to be that bride, the bride who will co-rule with Him throughout eternity. Revelation 21:9 speaks of the bride, the Lamb's wife. The Epistle of Paul to the Ephesians even says we have been raised up and made to sit together with Him (Jesus) in Heavenly places. *"But God, who is rich in mercy, because of His great love with which He loved us, even when we were dead in trespasses, made us alive together with Christ (by grace you have been saved), and raised us up together, and made us sit together in the heavenly places in Christ Jesus, that in the ages to come He might show the exceeding riches of His grace in His kindness toward us in Christ Jesus."* Ephesians 2:4-7

What else can this mean but joint rulership? This rulership position is also referred to in 1 Corinthians 6 where Paul addresses going to court against your fellow Christian. *"Do you not know that the saints will judge the world? And if the world will be judged by you, are you unworthy to judge the smallest matters? Do you not know that we shall judge angels? How much more, things that pertain to this life?* 1 Cor. 6:2-3. It's an amazing revelation. May God help us to understand all He has done for us and given us. – December 19, 2021

NOTES

12. If You've Seen Me, You've Seen the Father

Jesus made this statement in John 14:9 when one of His disciples said "show us the Father." *Jesus said to him, "Have I been with you so long, and yet you have not known Me, Philip? He who has seen Me has seen the Father; so how can you say, 'Show us the Father'?*

Please realize the context of this. These men had been with Him for a long time, witnessing supernatural events on a regular basis. They saw Him rebuke a storm, walk on water, cast out demons from people, heal all manners of sickness and disease, raise dead people, provide ample food where there was none for people who came to hear Him teach, find a coin in a fish's mouth with which to pay their taxes and curse a tree and it withered. So, for one of them to say show us the Father would indicate someone wasn't paying attention!! Jesus WAS showing them the Father!

Hebrews 1:3 says of Jesus, the Word, the Son of God, *"who being the brightness of His* (God's) *glory and the express image of His person, and upholding all things by the word of His power, when He had by Himself purged our sins, sat down at the right hand of the Majesty on high,..."*

The Passion Translation says it like this: *"The Son is the dazzling radiance of God's splendor, the exact expression of God's true nature–His mirror image! He holds the universe together and expands it by the mighty power of His spoken word. He accomplished for us the complete cleansing of sins and then took His seat on the highest throne at the right hand of the majestic One."*

So if we want to know what God is like, we must look at Jesus. The character of God Himself is directly illustrated to us in the life and character of Jesus Christ. People get confused when they read the Old Testament and see a God who is in favor of killing people. That discussion is for another day. Jesus is the express image of God Himself.

So what was Jesus like? I think most of us are familiar with the bible stories of what He did while He was alive on the earth. 1 John 3:8 says His purpose in coming to the earth was to *"destroy the works of the devil."* In order to do this, He cast demons out of people and healed all manner of sickness and disease. Does this witness to you that God loves people? I mean, really loves people. It does to me. Is it His will that we be sick? It doesn't look like it to me. As a second witness to this fact, did you know the body was created to heal itself? Well, who created our bodies? This tells me that sickness is not God's will, otherwise, why would our bodies work to heal themselves?

Sickness is a thief and a killer. *"The thief does not come except to steal, and to kill, and to destroy. I have come that they may have life, and that they may have it more abundantly."* John 10:10. Sickness steals your time, your attention, and your money. Sickness is not abundant life, which is what He promised.

So, we can conclude, just from the John 14:9 and Hebrews 1:3 verses, that Jesus perfectly represented the character and the will of God for mankind. So why don't we see people experiencing more of this? Because they don't believe it. The

benefits of God depend on faith in His promises. They won't
just land on us.

Believe that God wants you well today! Jesus has plainly
showed us that is God's desire. He has destroyed the works of
the devil. He's a good God who wants good things for His
people. We need to put our faith in that truth.

*Dear Jesus, We are dense in our understanding of who You really
are. Illuminate our hearts today as we ponder Your character and
Your power as Your Word says. — December 28, 2021*

NOTES

13. The Gates of Hell Shall Not Prevail

There has always been a question in my mind about Matthew 16:18. *"And I also say to you that you are Peter, and on this rock I will build My church, and the gates of Hades shall not prevail against it."* Perhaps some of my misunderstanding comes from my Catholic background, which always said Peter was the pope, but that is not the part I had questions about. I have long ago discarded the Catholic teaching as the truth of this passage. This scripture is about so much more.

In the context of when Jesus says this, He has just asked the disciples who men said He was. Then He asked, Who do you say I am? He was asking this question of a group of men who had been with Him for some time. They were witnesses to all of the supernatural events that followed Him. I have spoken of these elsewhere. In response, Peter blurted out, *"You are the Christ, the Son of the living God."* Matthew 16:16.

That was the right answer! Jesus commended him for it, saying that Peter was blessed because he had not learned that from a man, but from the Father in Heaven. He then goes on to state in the above passage, that on this rock, which was revelation from Heaven, He would build His church. It is the revealing from Heaven of the truth that is the "rock" in this passage. When a person receives this type of revelation about anything from God's Kingdom, it convinces them. When God reveals something to you, you are not easily shaken from it.

You know down in your "knower," your heart, that this is TRUTH. We need this certainty in our lives. This is what Peter encountered in this incident. The Spirit of God revealed to him personally in his heart, that Jesus was the Christ, the One sent from God. He was convinced and Jesus commended him for that.

So this "rock" of revelation from Heaven is what the gates of hell shall not prevail against. This "rock" is unmovable. It has always bugged me, though, because the word prevail, in my mind, seems to be an offensive term. It speaks to me of moving forward and attempting to do battle with something.

It is true that hell does oppose the teaching and the receiving of the Word of God. Jesus talked about how when the word is taught, opposition comes to steal it from those who hear it. This opposition challenges us with, "has God really said?"

But gates are a stationary item; they don't assault anyone. They, in and of themselves, don't move. They hold things in. They guard and protect territory. Recently I heard a teacher say that…then the skies parted and the heavens opened…and I saw.

Gates are stationary; they keep things in. But Jesus said the gates guarding territory held by dark forces cannot prevail or remain standing, or win or prove superior against a church that is ADVANCING, moving, pushing forward with truth to take that territory (meaning persuading people) in the culture.

In other words, those gates will not stand when the church says, no, we will not concede defeat to the devil's works of darkness in our culture. We will not concede to ungodly teaching in our schools. We will not concede to ungodly laws and rules and edicts put on us. We will not concede to lawlessness. We will oppose it.

The CHURCH is supposed to assault the gates of hell, the places of darkness in our culture through prayer, speaking out, and doing the actual works of Jesus, and the gates which are guarding the darkness will fold and crumble because they cannot prevail, they cannot stand against the onslaught of righteousness and truth. This is what Matthew 16:18 is speaking of. This is what was revealed from Heaven to me. It makes all the sense in the world now.
– December 28, 2021

NOTES

14. What Does it Mean, Jesus is the Light of the World?

What does light do? When you walk into a dark room and turn on a light switch, what happens? The darkness is not there anymore. It disappears. This is much more than an object lesson. It has spiritual applications also. The light exposes things that are hidden. If you are looking for something in the dark, will you not turn on a light so that you can find it?

In the book of Genesis, God separated the light from the darkness. He made nighttime and daytime. This is not only in the natural sense; it also teaches us about spiritual realities.

When Adam and Eve essentially kicked God out of the Garden of Eden through their disobedience, they teamed up with the devil and gave dominion over the earth to him. They sided with the devil through their sin. They switched teams. We too side with him when we sin. The powers of darkness were now in charge…for a while.

Where Man once had the task of ruling the earth, the disobedience of the Eden couple had now turned it over to satan. They were now under the rule of satan. The light, or the truth of God, was now left out of the earth realm. Adam and Eve's minds had become darkened under their new rulers, and this was passed down to all men born after that. Sin brought all kinds of evil into the world.

The apostle Paul made this statement in 2 Corinthians 4:3-4: *"But even if our gospel is veiled, it is veiled to those who are perishing, whose minds the god of this age has blinded, who do not believe, lest the light of the gospel of the glory of Christ, who is the image of God, should shine on them."*

Let's establish that spirits, any spirit, be it God or satan, need a human body to operate through. This is because man, the tri-part human being, was given the earth and told to rule over it. He was given that authority. *"The heaven, even* the *heavens, are the LORD's; But the earth He has given to the children of men. Psalm 115:16.* So in order to legally operate here, a spirit has to have the cooperation of a human being. This is spiritual law.

This is what happened in the Garden. Because of the way God set everything up, He actually needed permission from Man to work in the earth. But God already had a plan to get back dominion for his created man. God knew beforehand that this would happen and had already prepared a way to restore mankind to His original intent.

We see in the Gospels that when Jesus cast demonic spirits out of a person, thereby releasing the person from their influence, the spirits went into pigs at one point, but they made the pigs crazy and they jumped over a cliff and died. So it is possible for them to occupy animals also, but they prefer men because of their rulership status.

We see Jesus in the Gospels being tempted by satan to follow his instructions, but Jesus overcame him by using the word of God against the devil. Jesus used the truth of the word of God and satan then left Him alone for awhile. For us too, the word of God, the truth of God, is our weapon to defeat the lies of satan.

Our enemy, satan, opposes God, the word of God, and the people of God. He hates human beings in general. So because Jesus has come and totally demoralized and defeated him, making a spectacle of him openly, his only power is deception, lies, etc. and everything that opposes the truth of God's word. Colossians 2:15 *"Having disarmed principalities and powers, He made a public spectacle of them, triumphing over them in it."*

The truth is the light that has been given to us so that we can navigate in this dark world. And how important is it to know that truth! Without it, we are stumbling in the dark. And here is truth, *"For this purpose the Son of God was manifested, that He might destroy the works of the devil."* 1 John 3:8.

Scripture says we have been transferred from darkness (the lies, deceptions) into the kingdom of light. Adam and Eve walked in light and truth before they sinned, communing freely with God. After they sinned, they hid from Him because they were afraid. They had never been afraid until that moment.

The unknown author of Psalms 119 writes, *"Your word is a lamp to my feet And a light to my path." Psalm 119:105.* And it truly is!

As we begin this new year of 2022, let us determine to pursue the light of God and get as much understanding as we can so that we can navigate the world we live in and cooperate with God's plan for mankind. – January 1, 2022

NOTES

15. Don't Throw Away Your Love

According to the bible, faith works by love. Galatians 5:6 *"For in Christ Jesus neither circumcision nor uncircumcision avails anything, but faith working through love."*

The Passion Translation of that verse says: *"When you're placed into the Anointed One and joined to Him, circumcision and religious obligations can benefit you nothing. All that matters now is living in the faith that is activated and brought to perfection by love."*

1 Corinthians 13:1-6 gives us a clear definition of love. It is the supernatural, God kind of love, unconditional, never failing, always patient and kind, long suffering, doesn't envy, isn't puffed up, doesn't behave rudely, doesn't seek its own, rejoices in the truth, bears all things, believes all things, hopes all things and endures all things. It's pretty amazing!

I want to address the effects of disappointment that I have observed in my own life and in the life of others in this post. Disappointment is a fact of life. We all have and/or will experience it. We all have hopes to see certain things happen and when it doesn't, we are disappointed. Disappointment can kill the kind of love spoken of in 1 Corinthians 13. We stop "bearing all things, believing all things, hoping all things and enduring all things." Disappointment in a marriage can cause a spouse to turn to another person. Disappointment in how children turn out can cause a family to turn away from them, to stop being patient and long suffering.

Disappointment leads to deception. I have seen this. Disappointment moves one away from faith, away from believing all things, bearing, hoping and enduring all things. Committing ourselves to living in the unconditional God kind of love, on the other hand, causes us to be able to see truth. We won't be deceived. We will see clearly as God sees because we rise spiritually to a higher place. We will fulfill the will of God. We will make right decisions, if we are committed to love and to truth in all things.

Examine your heart today. Where in your life have you been disappointed in someone? Have you put distance between you and that person because you were disappointed in something they did? Sometimes emotional distance is called for when dealing with a manipulative person so that you can examine things further in order to see the truth and how you are to deal with the person, but it doesn't mean you throw away your love and give up on them. It is easy, especially as a parent, to feel responsible for children's lives and the choices they make, but this is not what God has called us to.

As the eldest child in a family who was often called upon to "take care" of other younger children, I find this to be a trait that I have to watch in myself. I feel for others and the situations they find themselves in, but I cannot live their lives for them. I would gladly help them find an answer if they were open to that. Too often they are not. But I don't stop loving or caring for them.

We must push through disappointment and disillusionment of heart and come back to hope and to love, to prayer and to faith in God. *"Why are you cast down, O my soul? And why are you disquieted within me? Hope in God, for I shall yet praise Him For the help of His countenance."* Psalm 42:5.

The answer to the disillusionments of life is never to turn to outward things or people. The answer is always Jesus. Let us resolve today on this first day of the new year of 2022 to hold onto love, and to faith in God and to hope. – January 1, 2022

NOTES

16. Psalm 91: A Prayer of Protection

God wants to protect His people in the midst of the chaos of our day. Psalm 91 is a confession, an assertion of His desire and of His love and protection for us. I always pray this to the Lord as a statement and confession of my faith in His word. You can too! He will keep us!

"I dwell in the secret place of the Most High and abide under the shadow of the Almighty.

"I shall say of the Lord, You are my refuge and my fortress, my God, in You do I trust.

"Surely You shall deliver me from the snare of the fowler and from the noisome pestilence.

"You shall cover me with Your feathers and under Your wings do I find refuge.

"I shall not be afraid of the terror by night, nor of the arrow that flies by day, nor of the pestilence that walks in darkness, nor of the destruction that lays waste at noonday.

"A thousand shall fall at my side and ten thousand at my right hand, but it shall not come near me.

"Only with my eyes will I behold and see the reward of the wicked.

"Because I have made You, even the Most High, my habitation, there shall no evil befall me,

"Neither shall any plague come near my dwelling.

"For You shall give your angels charge over me to keep me in all my ways.

"They shall bear me up in their hands, lest I dash my foot against a stone.

"I shall tread upon the lion and the adder, the young lion and dragon shall I trample underfoot.

"Because I have set my love upon You, therefore You shall deliver me.

"You have set me on high, because I have known Your name.

"I shall call upon You and You will answer me.

"You will be with me in trouble, you will deliver me and honor me.

"With long life will You satisfy me and show me Your salvation."—
January 20, 2022

NOTES

17. Signs of the Times We Live in

For the past few years in Illinois, a satanist group has put a display with their "baby" Baphomet (it looks like a demon) in a manger in the capital building in Springfield during the Christmas season. Baphomet is a goat-like satanic deity, and the display was set up next to a traditional Christian Nativity display. News media reported that members of the Satanic Temple of Illinois stood around proclaiming "Hail, Satan!" and giving explanations of their peaceful, loving intent. A few steps away, Christian protesters from the American Society for the Defense of Tradition, Family and Property were kneeling and praying near the Christian nativity scene. They displayed signs with slogans such as "Satan Has No Rights" and "Begone, Satan! Mary Crushes the Serpent."

In January, it was announced that a school in Moline, Ill. was going to host a "satan club." the club claims it won't be evangelizing, but since we know satan is a liar, what good is that promise? I have since read of another school doing this also.

What do these events tell us? These events are a "tell." And what they "tell" me is that satan is not afraid of the church. He is so not afraid that he comes right out in the open. What's next? Will he don a red suit and horns and carry a pitchfork and walk among us openly and visibly? It looks like we are almost at that point.

This is a challenge to the church. He's not hiding anymore. He is openly defiant of God and God's people. We may see more weird stuff as time goes on.

This reminds me of the story of the giant Philistine Goliath. He kept the armies of Israel in fear because of his size and ferocity as he challenged Israel to send someone out to fight him. No one would because they had forgotten who they were, people with a covenant with the God of the universe.

The church is a lot like David, the 17-year-old who finally did take on the challenge. The church LOOKS pretty weak and passive and unable to challenge the "giants" in our society. Goliath wasn't afraid of David at all. He was actually offended when the lad came out to challenge him. But that's where Goliath made his biggest mistake and it cost him his head. Because of his arrogance and pride, he could not discern what was actually happening.

What Goliath didn't know, is that David knew his identity in God. The anointing, glory, and power of the Lord God rested on that young man. Goliath made a very big error in judgment...

The church too has the anointing, the glory, and the power of the Lord in them, and yet, satan has no qualms about challenging us. Granted, he's not as smart as God, but he knows when he sees weakness, and I think he is calling the church out on that, daring us to engage him. I believe most Christians don't yet understand that the power that raised Christ from the dead dwells in our mortal bodies. *"Greater is He that is in you than he (devil) that is in the world."* 1 John 4:4. We have the power, the anointing, and the authority given to us by Christ to deal with these issues. Jesus is the Head of the universe; we are on the right side of this thing! We are supposed to be ruling with spiritual weapons, which will bring change to our circumstances. People of courage must unite and attack evil, not only with spiritual weapons, but by also speaking out openly at injustice and wrongdoing. Then we will see satan withdraw and his works demolished.

Jesus came to destroy the works of the devil. Believers need to be about that same business in whatever capacity God has called them to. 1 John 3:8 *"…for this purpose the Son of God was manifested, that He might destroy the works of the devil."*

Are you born again? Is Jesus your Savior? That will take you only so far; you are cleansed from sin. But is Jesus your LORD? He is the Lord of the universe right now. He is the Boss. He sits on the throne at the right hand of God. If He is your Lord, that means surrender to His will and plan. That means you are now enlisted in God's army and are now in the war for men's souls. You are also now a part of the Kingdom of God and aligned with the greatest power in earth and Heaven on your side.

The times we live in call for surrender to the King.

Romans 10:9-10 *"If you confess with your mouth the Lord Jesus and believe in your heart that God has raised Him from the dead, you will be saved. For with the heart one believes unto righteousness and with the mouth confession is made unto salvation."* – January 29, 2022

NOTES

18. Is the Word You Hear Profiting You?

This scripture has been much on my mind the past few weeks…

"The gospel was preached to us as well as to them; but the word which they heard did not profit them, not being mixed with faith in those who heard it." Hebrews 4:2

This scripture refers to the first generation of the Israelites whom Moses led out of the land of Egypt. God set them free from their oppressors. They had been in Egypt 400 years. After Joseph's death, over time, a Pharaoh arose who did not know Joseph and it was under him that the Israelites became slaves in Egypt, forced to do the hardest of labor.

When Moses led them out of their prison, the people saw great wonders of deliverance from God, demonstrations of His care for them. I'm speaking of the Red Sea crossing, as they walked over on dry land, but when Pharaoh's army tried to do it, the sea swallowed them up. The people saw their enemies totally overthrown. There were times they didn't have water, He made water come from a rock for the few million of them. He gave them supernatural food in the wilderness. Psalm 78 recounts the early history of the nation. But yet they did not remember His power, vs. 42 says. They continued to grumble and complain in unbelief.

Egypt is a type of the world. We have also been delivered from the ways of the world (sin). We have been given promises, a type of Promised Land, just like they were. We are told these promises are for us. 2 Peter 1:2. They were told the Promised Land was theirs. But ten men were able to sway the whole nation and convince them they could not have it. The devil loves to persuade us too that we can't have what God has promised us. Will we let him gaslight us? Will we let the devil bamboozle us and keep us from our promised land, a better life? We need to press forward in faith. All the promises of God are yes and amen! 2 Corinthians 1:20

That first generation of Israel eventually died in the wilderness because they did not believe the promises of God. They never obtained what God had promised them. The word God spoke to them did not profit them, because they didn't embrace it with faith. They had faith in what the ten spies said.

There were two spies who said the people could have the Promised Land, but their voices were drowned out. Those two also didn't get to enter the Promised Land until later, but they had the privilege (I believe) of training the next generation and getting them ready to enter in. Joshua became their leader. The next generation, the children of those who did not believe, were the ones we see at the beginning of the book of Joshua. They were the ones who went forth in faith to obtain what God had promised. Everyone knows the story of Jericho.

As one keeps reading in the book of Joshua, we see they weren't perfect. They made mistakes, but they continued to steadily conquer and take the Promised Land. Every victory builds faith, even for us. That history is important. Later we see that succeeding generations were disobedient and experienced the consequences. But God never gave up on them, continually raising up leaders as the people cried out to Him.

Are we mixing the promises of God with our faith in order to obtain them from God? This life of faith is not a passive one. He requires us to actively participate with our faith and actions. I always say, the promises don't just land on us. We have to participate. We have to pursue it, because we live in this earth with a devil who is always resisting and hindering God's will from being done "on earth as it is in Heaven." That is what we pursue…God's will being done on earth as it is in Heaven.

Let us not be like those that Hebrews 4 speaks of. Let us always mix our faith with what God is speaking to us. We CAN have what He has promised us! All the promises are yes and Amen!

2 Peter 1:2 *"…as His divine power has given to us all things that pertain to life and godliness, through the knowledge of Him who called us by glory and virtue, by which have been given to us exceedingly great and precious promises, that through these you may be partakers of the divine nature, having escaped the corruption that is in the world through lust."* March 6, 2022

NOTES

19. What Does the Word "Prayer" Mean to You?

What does that word mean to you? Does it conjure up images of kneeling with a rosary and repeating pre-written words, such as my own experience as a young Catholic girl? Or does it remind you of being with a group, with everyone totally silent and nothing spoken out loud? Or does it conjure up the image of a group holding hands and standing in a circle with someone speaking out loud as others agree and nod their heads in agreement? Or are you reminded of a group speaking loudly and boldly, even all at once sometimes, boisterous, with strange words mixed with English that provide an atmosphere of liveliness and strangeness all at the same time? I have experienced all of these with different groups of Christians. Whatever your image is, I submit that we all have a somewhat different viewpoint and definition of what "prayer" actually is.

Personal prayer time is different than coming together in a group. By its very nature, it must be. The word "prayer," by dictionary definition, means a solemn request for help or expression of thanks addressed to God or an object of worship. Breaking it down even more, I see that "prayer" can be a petition for yourself, where intercession is usually when one steps in on behalf of others. I have gone through the scriptures to get a deeper understanding of this thing we call "prayer." I think I may have to adjust my own understanding as I see prayer perhaps being used as a catchall word, but there are many other aspects to the believer's relationship with God that could fall under that comprehensive label. I personally need the specificity of each aspect in order to understand what others are speaking of when they use the word.

Since the Bible is my go-to source for all things pertaining to life and godliness, as Peter says, 1 Timothy 2:1 says *"Therefore I exhort first of all that supplications, prayers, intercessions, and giving of thanks be made for all men,"* Right here we see four different things listed, but all would come under the heading of "prayer," if we are referring to relationship with God. This passage is speaking specifically of "prayer" on behalf of others.

If you were raised in church, the definition of prayer that you most likely have from childhood is what is in you and is the image you understand. I was raised as a little Catholic girl. We knelt to pray and used rosary beads to keep track of how many prayers of a certain type we said. I always lost count, though. The image of prayer implanted in my young mind was repetition of certain prayers over and over as penance for sin. Today, as one who is committed to scriptures as my guide in life, I see prayer as much more than that childhood image, yet the word still always conjures up petitioning God more than anything else.

I am working on expanding my definition of "prayer." I would submit to you that all aspects of Christian worship may come under that comprehensive heading, but with more specificity. There is worship, extolling the virtues of God and loving on Him. One can either speak it or think it or sing it. I think thanksgiving goes along with this. Dancing makes our physical body feel alive and, I believe is also a way to worship God. King David danced with all his might, it says in

2 Samuel 6:14. He was excited about what God had done for him, and he celebrated with dancing.

There is praying in the spirit (as Jude 1:20 and 1 Cor. 14:2 talks about), building ourselves up on our most holy faith or speaking mysteries unto God. There is petition and supplication, asking God to do things, usually on our own behalf. I believe intercession is petition on behalf of others. Abraham interceded in the book of Genesis on behalf of Lot to deliver him when he (Abraham) learned that Sodom and Gomorrah were to be destroyed because of their sin.

In the New Testament, Peter was slated for execution by Herod in Acts 12, "But constant prayer was offered to God for him by the church" (Acts 12:5) and Peter was set free by an angel. I would call that fervent intercession!

Another aspect is what we might term as decreeing or declaring. In the book of Job, we see a powerful statement that says, "You will also declare a thing, And it will be established for you; So light will shine on your ways." Job 22:28. The King James Version says decree instead of declare, but they have the same meaning. This is speaking the words of God aloud with authority, or commanding, such as when Jesus said to the fig tree, "Let no fruit grow on you ever again," in Matthew 21:19 and Mark 11:15. He later tells his disciples, "whoever shall say to this mountain, be thou removed and does not doubt, it shall be done for him." Mark 20-23. This is an example of decreeing or declaring.

Meditation could be considered another type of prayer, as we read His word aloud and speak it so that our hearts can hear it. Faith comes by hearing the word of God. If you are having any trouble in your faith, I would suggest finding the scriptures for your situation, then speak them aloud, many times if you need to. We can build our faith in His word this way. This is how we renew our mind to think like God thinks and drive out the negative thoughts that come to us. Remember, we are made in the image of God. When God created the earth and everything in it, God spoke words first, then He saw it and said it was all good.

This is not a comprehensive study on prayer by any means, but just a few things I have learned in my journey with God. In the end, there are many expressions of our relationship with God. It's all good! - March 12, 2022

NOTES

20. Angels Don't Rule in the Age to Come...We Do

For He has not put the world to come...in subjection to angels. Hebrews 2:5

"Do you not know that the saints will judge the world? And if the world will be judged by you, are you unworthy to judge the smallest matters? Do you not know that we shall judge angels? How much more, things that pertain to this life?- 1 Corinthians 6:2-3

The plan of God always was that man would rule over the earth. That was the domain given to him. We see this in the scriptures. In Genesis 1:28. God commissioned His created man and wife to "have dominion over the earth."

In Psalms 8:3-6, the Psalmist says, *"When I consider Your heavens, the work of Your fingers, The moon and the stars, which You have ordained,*
What is man that You are mindful of him, And the son of man that You visit him?
You have made him to have dominion over the works of Your hands; For You have made him a little lower than the angels, And You have crowned him with glory and honor. You have put all things under his feet,"

It may be hard to believe, but God has never changed His mind about this purpose. It's just that there has been opposition to His plan ever since the first couple sinned in the Garden of Eden. Our spiritual enemy, satan, does not want God, or men and women to be successful. He wants to destroy people. He fights the desires of God everywhere he can. That is why we see the increased warfare of our time. Men have strayed further and further away from God and become totally lawless. The warfare is against everything that is good and right.

But it was Jesus who said the gates of hell would not prevail against the church in Matthew 16:18. So it is the Church, the body and expression of Christ in the earth, who offensively assault the gates of hell that this promise is for. The forces of righteousness can and will prevail. It may take some time. I'm not talking about Christians taking over the world per se, but I am talking about God's influence increasingly coming into the earth, into our nation, our states, our counties and towns, in a greater way than it ever has to affect our world and our society that so desperately needs it right now. Let this be our mission and our aim. We are here to influence. We are ambassadors of Heaven.

Of the Church, which consists of those who have experienced salvation, Ephesians says, God has *"raised us up together, and made us sit together in the heavenly places in Christ Jesus, that in the ages to come He might show the exceeding riches of His grace in His kindness toward us in Christ Jesus."* Ephesians 2:6-7.

Man is God's prized creation, His crowning glory. We have been made in His image. We indeed are special. We are co-heirs with Christ. If we are saved, we carry the Light of the World inside of us.

Let's determine to let that glory, that image of God and His goodness, be revealed to those around us. We are in training!

Because of the darkness in the present world, our lights will be brighter than ever. --- March 19, 2022

NOTES

21. The Eyes of the Lord

2 Chronicles 16:9 *"For the eyes of the LORD run to and fro throughout the whole earth, to show Himself strong on behalf of those whose heart is loyal to Him…"*

The context of this verse is this….a seer came to a king of Judah to chastise him for relying on the help of another king instead of on God alone. The seer gives the king an example of a previous battle when the Lord had delivered the enemy into his hand and then goes on to make this statement about the eyes of the Lord. This statement is a true statement that all of us as God's children can embrace as a promise for our own lives.

How would you like to have the Lord show Himself strong on your behalf? You can. He loves you and wants to prove Himself to you, to show Himself strong on your behalf. I have had several dramatic near misses in "near accidents" where I knew the Lord was working on my behalf. Life can be a series of near misses sometimes and I am always glad to see Him work on my behalf, especially in a possible car accident! I have been saved several times!

I will share some more verses from the bible that run in this same vein. There are a few in Proverbs and the Psalms.

Psalms 34:15 *"The eyes of the LORD are on the righteous, And His ears are open to their cry."*

Proverbs 5:21 *"For the ways of man are before the eyes of the LORD, And He ponders all his paths."*

Proverbs 15:3 *"The eyes of the LORD are in every place, Keeping watch on the evil and the good.*

Proverbs 22:12 *"The eyes of the LORD preserve knowledge, But He overthrows the words of the faithless."* I like this one too.

The New Testament has a verse about the eyes of the Lord in 1 Peter 3:12, *"For the eyes of the Lord are on the righteous and His ears are open to their prayers….*

These are great promises, to know that He is actually looking around searching for someone to show Himself strong for, and that He is drawn to us when our hearts are drawn to Him, is comforting in the dark world that we presently live in. It's dark here, but it's even darker in other countries. I believe God is always looking for faith. It gets His attention; He is drawn to it. His power is drawn to it. He loves all of us, but not all of us love Him. There are bible stories of how faith drew His attention and His power.

"Then those who feared the LORD spoke to one another, And the LORD listened and heard them; So a book of remembrance was written before Him For those who fear the LORD And who meditate on His name. 'They shall be Mine," says the LORD of hosts, "On the day that I make them My jewels. And I will spare them As a man spares his own son who serves him.' Malachi 3:16-17. I love this verse. – March 25, 2022

NOTES

22. Are You Fully Persuaded?

Romans 4:18-21 *"Against all hope, Abraham in hope believed and so became the father of many nations, just as he had been told, "So shall your offspring be." Without weakening in his faith, he acknowledged the decrepitness of his body (since he was about a hundred years old) and the lifelessness of Sarah's womb. Yet he did not waver through disbelief in the promise of God, but was strengthened in his faith and gave glory to God, being fully persuaded that God was able to do what He had promised."* Berean Study Bible

If I were to ask you, do you believe the bible, most Christians and perhaps even those who don't attend church would say yes. But take them to a particular scripture, such as the story of a 100 year old man having a baby with a 90 year old wife, and you may find resistance. How about a virgin conceiving a child outside the usual human method of conception? How about the story of a 17 year old boy taking down a nine foot giant with one stone in a slingshot? There are all sorts of stories and actions in the bible that people don't see how they could happen, and they are not fully persuaded of their reality. It goes against their natural thinking.

There's one instance when Israel was in the middle of a battle (Joshua 10), and Joshua asked God to make the sun stand still to give him more daylight. The sun really stood still and did not go down for a day. Don't ask me to explain scientifically how that happened. I just know that God did it because the story is recorded and He is the one who made the universe, the earth and everything in it, so I'm convinced He knows what He's doing.

Faith is being fully persuaded of something no matter what circumstances appear before your natural eyes. I have written before about David's victory over Goliath and how David wasn't looking at the circumstances. How did a 17 year old nobody defeat a nine foot tall fierce battle-hardened warrior? David's confidence came from the covenant he was **fully persuaded** he had with God. He was **confident** God was backing him up. Are you confident God is backing you up?

The bible in Hebrews 11:1 defines faith this way, "*Now faith is the substance of things hoped for, the evidence of things not seen.*" NKJV.

The Amplified bible says it like this, "*Now faith is the assurance (title deed, confirmation) of things hoped for (divinely guaranteed), and the evidence of things not seen [the conviction of their reality — faith comprehends as fact what cannot be experienced by the physical senses].*"

The dictionary defines faith this way: trust, belief, confidence, conviction; optimism, hopefulness, hope. And trust is defined as confidence, belief, faith, certainty, assurance, conviction, credence; reliance. I define faith as being fully persuaded or fully convinced. You just know that you know. It is definitely more than hope or hopefulness, which implies uncertainty. Hebrews 11:1 seems to agree with that, defining them as related, but two different things, one building on the other.

Are you fully persuaded that your sins were completely paid for by Jesus Christ, the Son of God, on the cross? How do you know that? Yes, it's written in the bible, but even that is just the starting point. How do you know that **you** have salvation?

Because Romans 10:9-10 says *"that if you confess with your mouth Jesus as Lord and believe in your heart that God raised Him from the dead, you will be saved, for with the heart a person believes, resulting in righteousness, and with the mouth he confesses, resulting in salvation,"* and you have exercised faith in that. You have met the requirements of that scripture and you are *fully persuaded* it is true! All the promises of God are yes and amen.

Faith (being fully persuaded or convinced) is how we receive everything from God.

"But without faith it is impossible to please Him, for he who comes to God must believe that He is, and that He is a rewarder of those who diligently seek Him." Hebrews 11:6. Our God **is** a good God. – March 27, 2022

NOTES

Katherine Sands is a freelance writer and artist who currently works as the editor of a local newspaper and website. She has been published in a national magazine and is the author of the first four Dogtags and Pearls books and the author of three children's books: A Tale of Two Lambs. The ABCs of Created Things, and A Tale of Two Prophets. She also illustrated the last two children's books.

Katherine and her husband David reside in Carmi, Ill.